AF266789

What do I need to Start a Photography Business

How to Start a Photography Business from Home

by Adler Taylor

TABLE OF CONTENTS

Copyright © 2020 MahoneyProducts

DEDICATION

This book is dedicated to Stephanie Tam
A good friend, a blessing from God.

ACKNOWLEDGMENTS

I WOULD LIKE TO ACKNOWLEDGE ALL THE
HARD WORK OF THE MEN AND WOMEN OF THE
UNITED STATES MILITARY, WHO RISK THEIR
LIVES ON A DAILY BASIS, TO MAKE THE WORLD
A SAFER PLACE.

Disclaimer

This book was written as a guide to starting a business. As with any other high yielding action, starting a business has a certain degree of risk. This book is not meant to take the place of accounting, legal, financial or other professional advice. If advice is needed in any of these fields, you are advised to seek the services of a professional.

While the author has attempted to make the information in this book as accurate as possible, no guarantee is given as to the accuracy or currency of any individual item. Laws and procedures related to business are constantly changing.

Therefore, in no event shall Brian Mahoney or MahoneyProducts Publishers be liable for any special, indirect, or consequential damages or any damages whatsoever in connection with the use of the information herein provided.

All Rights Reserved

No part of this book may be used or reproduced in any manner whatsoever without the written permission of the author.

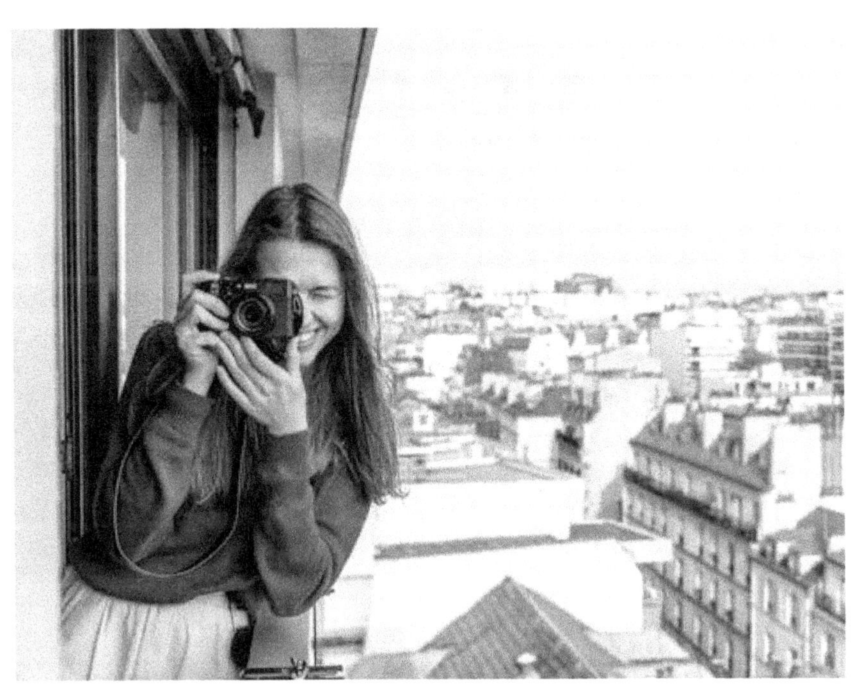

Chapter 1

Photographer Job Overview

Photographer Job Overview

What Photographers Do

Photographers are usually creative people with a good level of technical expertise to use cameras to take images of objects or events. Many photographers stand or walk and can carry heavy equipment.

Photographers usually:

* Promote their services to genterate business

* Plan the setting for the photographs

* Set up lighting equipment

* Use tested formulas for commercial level photos

* Use lighting to optimize the best photograph

* Use top quality photography software

* Keep a portfolio of their work for future clients

Photographer Job Overview

Film cameras used to be the standard, but today the majority of photographers use digital cameras to get electronic images. Electronic images and be edited on a computer. Images are stored on memory cards or computer hard drives and even flash drives. Once the image is on a storage device, photography software can then be used to manipulate and improve the image. With high quality printers, great photographic images can then be created. According to Techradar.com and Digital Camera Review these are some of the top digital cameras.

Camera	Retail Price
Nikon D810	$2999.95
Canon EOS 5D Mark IV	$3,499.00
Fuji X-T2	$124.07
Nikon D500	$1,796.95
Sony Alpha A7r II	$2,949.99
Nikon D3300	$355.99
Panasonic Lumix LX100	$578.70
Olympus OM-D E-M10 II	$549.00
Panasonic Lumix ZS50 /TZ70	$331.00
Canon EOS Rebel T6i / 750D	$549.00
Panasonic Lumix FZ1000	$690.00

Photographer Job Overview

As you can see, they vary a great deal in price, which means almost anybody can afford to get started in freelance photography. Freelance photographers usually offer wedding, portait, framing and photo album services.

Self employed photographers also...

* Must promote their business

* Handle appointments

* Purchase supplies

* Set up equipment

* Keep Records

* Handle billing

* Pay business expenses

* Maybe hire and train employees

Photographer Job Overview

As a freelance photographer you can also teach photography classes and conduct photography workshops, in various learning institutions.

Here are some of the most popular types of photography:

* Portait Photography

* Commercial and Industry Photography

* Aerial Photography

* Scientific Photography

* PhotoJournalistic Photography

* Artistic Photography

* College Academic University Photography

Photographer Job Overview

Work Environment

According to the Bureau of Labor Statistics Photographers held about 124,900 jobs in the United States. Appoximately %60 were self-employed or freelance photographers.

The work environment for photographers depends on what field of photography they are in. Portrait photographers usually work inside of studios, and many times must travel to a school, corporate office or private residence. A photojournalist may have to travel all over the world, and often to dangerous places. Aerial photographers usually have to fly in planes or helicopters. Scientific photographers can also be tasked to travel internationally for their craft. While University and Artistic photography is usually done with less travel and In the comforts of Indoors.

Work Schedules

Thirty percent of photographers work part time with flexible work schedules. The season of the year often determines the demand for certain types of photography. Weddings usually occur in the spring and summer and amazing winter and fall photos have to be taken in those seasons.

Photographer Job Overview

Photographers who work for corporations may have the usual 9 to 5 hours, but news organizations may require a photographer at any time a story breaks.

How to Become a Photographer

You do not have to attend college to become a photographer. If you have talent with a camera, it is a good idea to keep a portfolio of your work and present it as proof of your skill. Many freelance websites have competition between freelancers to determine who they will hire.

Even though postsecondary education is not required, many photographers still learn a great deal of their craft by attending bachelor degree programs or vocational and technical school's certification programs.

Entry-level positions in photojournalism or in industrial or scientific photography generally require a college degree in photography or in a field related to the industry in which the photographer seeks employment. For example, classes in biology, medicine, or chemistry may be useful for scientific photographers.

Photographer Job Overview

Business, marketing, and accounting classes can be helpful for self-employed photographers.

To be a successful freelance photographer you should possess these skills...

* Artistic ability. A feel for lighting, color combinations and environment.

* Business skills. The ability to make a business plan, manage money and clients, and purchase the proper equipment and be able to focus and prioritize.

* Computer skills. With digital photography, it is now a must to be able to use photo editing software and have computer skills to post resumes and market your business with websites and even YouTube videos.

* Customer service skills. Whether it is dealing with difficult and demanding clients or unruly children or crying infants, the ability to show patience, compassion and a high level of professionalism is extremely important if you are going to be a successful freelancer who gets repeat work.

Photographer Job Overview

PAY

The wage for the top %10 of photographers was approximately $35.00 per hour. The median wage was approximately $15.25 per hour.

Freelance photographers can bid for projects that are on online job sites and set their own salary. They can also set up their own website and set the prices for each job according to industry standards.

Good word of mouth can keep a photographer in high demand and allow for a higher salary for fees.

JOB OUTLOOK

Jobs and employment for freelance photographers is expected to grow about %10 over the next 10 years. Family's get older and require new portrait photos, corporations need good photographers for their advertising campaigns, and as the population of the United States continues to increase, so will the demand for wedding photography. Creating and selling stock photography is another industry that internet marketing can help you to tap into.

The following chapters will assist you, in helping to put you in a better position to succeed as a freelance photographer. For every action there is a reaction. Use your personal power to take massive action for your individual success.

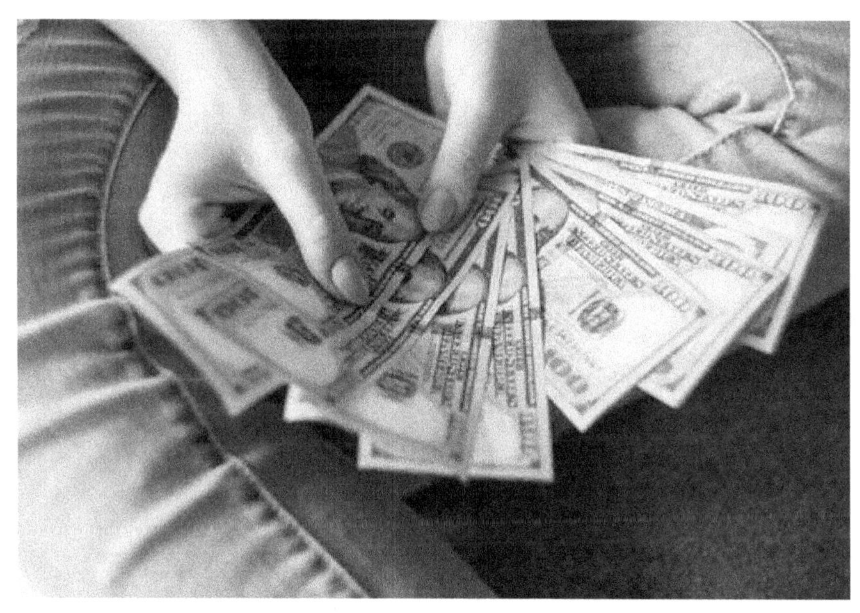

CHAPTER 2

Getting Started
Step by Step

Getting Started Step by Step

Getting Started in Your Home Business

There are thirty eight million home-based businesses in the United States alone.

Many people dream of the indepence and financial reward of having a home business. Unfortunately they let analysis paralysis stop them from taking action. This chapter is designed to give you a road map to getting started. The most difficult step in any journey is the first step.

Anthony Robbins created a program call Personal Power. I studied the program a long time ago, and I would summarize it, by saying you must figure out a way to motivate yourself(a powerful why) to take massive action without fear of failure.

2 Timothy 1:7 King James Version

"For God hath not given us the spirit of fear; but of power, and of love, and of a sound mind."

Getting Started Step by Step

STEP #1 MAKE AN OFFICE IN YOUR HOUSE

If you are serious about making money, then redo the man or woman cave and make a place for you t do business, uninterupted.

STEP #2 BUDGET OUT TIME FOR YOU BUSINE

If you already have a job, or if you have children, then they can take up a great deal of your time. No to mention well meaning friends who can use the phone and become time theifs. Budget time for you business and stick to it.

STEP #3 DECIDE ON THE TYPE OF BUSINESS

You don't have to be rigid, but begin with the end ir mine. You can become more flexible as you gain experience.

Getting Started Step by Step

STEP #4 LEGAL FORM FOR YOUR BUSINESS

The three basic legal forms are sole proprietorship, partnership, and corporation. Each one has it's advantages. Go to www.Sba.gov and learn about each and make a decision.

STEP #5 PICK A BUSINESS NAME AND REGISTER IT

One of the safest ways to pick a business name is to use your own name. Your own name is not copywrited. Just google Tom Cruise. However, always check with an Attorney or the proper legal authority when dealing with legal matters.

Getting Started Step by Step

STEP #6 WRITE A BUSINESS PLAN

This would seem like a no brainer. Even for a freelancer, you should have a business plan. In the NFL about seven headcoaches get fired every season. So in a very competetive business, a man with no head coaching experience got hired by the NFL's Philadelphia Eagles. His name was Andy Reid. He would become the most successful coach in the team's history. One of the reasons the owner hired him, was because he had a business plan the size of a telephone book. Your's does not need to be nearly that big, but if you plan for as much as possible, you are less likely to get rattled when things don't go as planned.

STEP #7 PROPER LICENSES & PERMITS

Go to city hall and find out what you need to do, to start a business.

Getting Started Step by Step

STEP #8 SELECT BUSINESS CARDS, STATIONERY, BROCHURES

This is one of the least expensive ways to not only start your business but to promote and network your business.

STEP #9 OPEN A BUSINESS CHECKING ACCOUNT

Having a separate business account makes it much easier to keep track of profit and expenses. This will come in very handy, whether you decide to do your taxes or hire out an professional.

STEP #10 TAKE SOME SORT OF ACTION TODAY!

This is not meant to be a comprehensive plan to start a business. It is meant to point you in the right direction to get started. You can go to the Small Business Administration for many free resources for starting your business. They even have a program(SCORE) that will give you access to many retired professionals who will advise you for free! www.score.org

Conclusion

As a freelancer you are not limited as you would be in the conventional workforce. Use this to your advantage. Many people, especially on the micro job websites don't care what your education is, they simply want somebody who can do the job they desire to be done. Many skill sets don't take four year degrees. Many technical institutes have risen up and proved that people can be trained professionals without taking other classes that don't relate to their chosen profession. With the massive library of training videos available on YouTube, you certainly can make money as a freelancer, having more than one skill set.

I have a complete set of training videos that teach you a completely zero cost way of not only marketing yourself, but any business you desire, on today's biggest marketplace. The Internet. Don't have a great day. Make it a great day. Make it a great life.

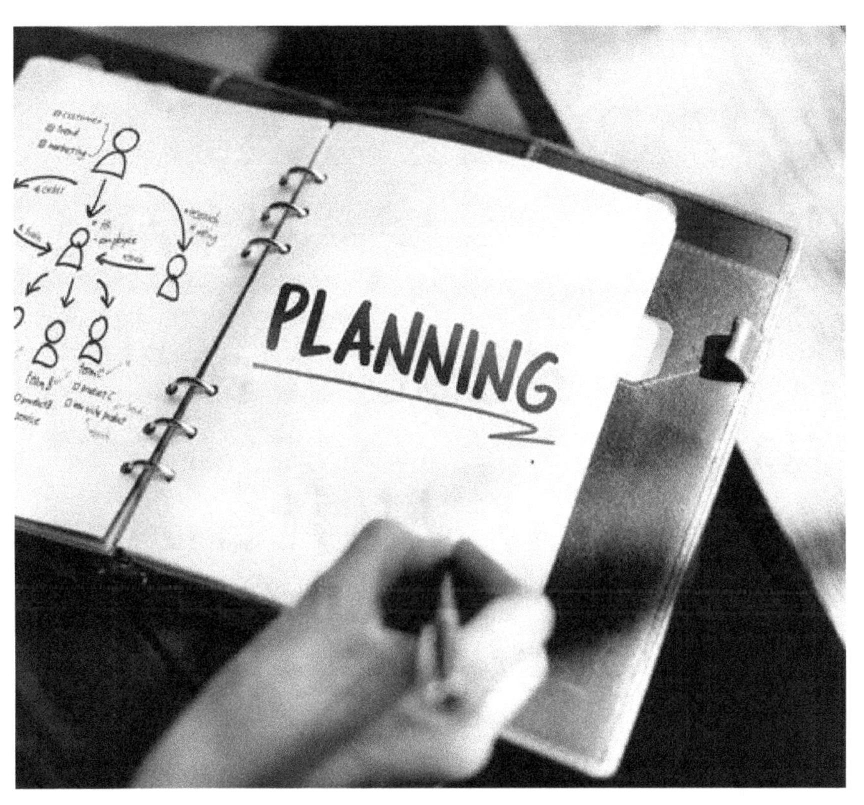

PLANNING

Chapter 3

Best Way
To Write A
Business Plan

How to Write a Business Plan

Millions of people want to know what is the secret to making money. Most have come to the conclusion that it is to start a business. So how do you start a business? The first thing you do to start a business is to create a business plan.

A business plan is a formal statement of a set of business goals, the reasons they are believed attainable, and the plan for reaching those goals. It may also contain background information about the organization or team attempting to reach those goals.

A professional business plan consists of eight parts.

1. Executive Summary

The executive summary is a very important part of your business plan. Many consider it the most important because this part of your plan gives a summary of the current state of your business, where you want to take it and why the business plan you have made will be a success. When requesting funds to start your business, the executive summary is a chance to get the attention of a possible investor.

2. Company Description

The company description part of your business plan gives a high level review of the different aspects of your business. This is like putting your elevator pitch into a brief summary that can help readers and possible investors quickly grasp the goal of your business and what will make it stand out, or what unique need it will fill.

3. Market Analysis

The market analysis part of your business plan should go into detail about your industries market and monetary potential. You should demonstrate detailed research with logical strategies for market penetration. Will you use low prices or high quality to penetrate the market?

4. Organization and Management

The Organization and Management section follows the Market Analysis. This part of the business plan will have your companies organizational structure, the type of business structure of incorporation, the ownership, management team and the qualifications of everyone holding these positions including the board of directors if necessary.

5. Service or Product Line

The Service or Product Line part of your business plan gives you a chance to describe your service or product. Focus on the benefits to the customers more than what the product or service does. For example, a air conditioner makes cold air. The benefit of the product is it cools down and makes customers more comfortable whether they are driving in bumper to bumper traffic or are sick and sitting in a nursing home. Air Conditioners fill a need that could mean the difference between life and death. Use this section to state what are the most important benefits of your product or service and what need it fills.

6. Marketing and Sales

Having a proven marketing plan is a essential element to the success of any business. Today online sales are dominating the marketplace. Present a strong internet marketing plan as well as social media plan. YouTube videos, Facebook Ads and Press Releases all can be part of your internet marketing plan. Passing out flyers and business cards are still an effective way to reach potential customers.

Use this part of your business plan to state your projected sales and how you came to that number. Do your research on similar companies for possible statistics on sales numbers.

7. Funding Request

When you write your Funding Request section of you business plan, be sure to be detailed and have documentation of the cost of supplies, building space, transportation, overhead and promotion of your business.

8. Financial Projections

The following is a list of the important financial statements to include in your business plan packet.

Historical Financial Data

Your historical financial data would be bank statements, balance sheets and possible collateral fo your loan.

Prospective Financial Data

The prospective financial data section of your business plan should show your potential growth within your industry, projecting out for at least the next five years.

You can have monthly or quarterly projections for th first year. Then project from year to year.

Inclin a ratio and trend analysis for all of your financial statements. Use colorful graphs to explain positive trends, as part of the financial projections section of your business plan.

How to Write a Business Plan

Appendix

The appendix should not be part of the main body of your business plan. It should only be provided on a need to know basis. Your business plan may be seen by a lot of people and you don't want certain information available to everybody. Lenders may need such information so you should have an appendix ready just in case.

The appendix would include:

Credit history (personal & business)

Resumes of key managers

Product pictures

Letters of reference

Details of market studies

Relevant magazine articles or book references

Licenses, permits or patents

Legal documents

Copies of leases

Building permits

Contracts

List of business consultants, including attorne
and accountant

Keep a record of who you allow to see your busines
plan.

Include a Private Placement Disclaimer. A Private
Placement Disclaimer is a private placement
memorandum (PPM) is a document focused mainly
on the possible downsides of an investment.

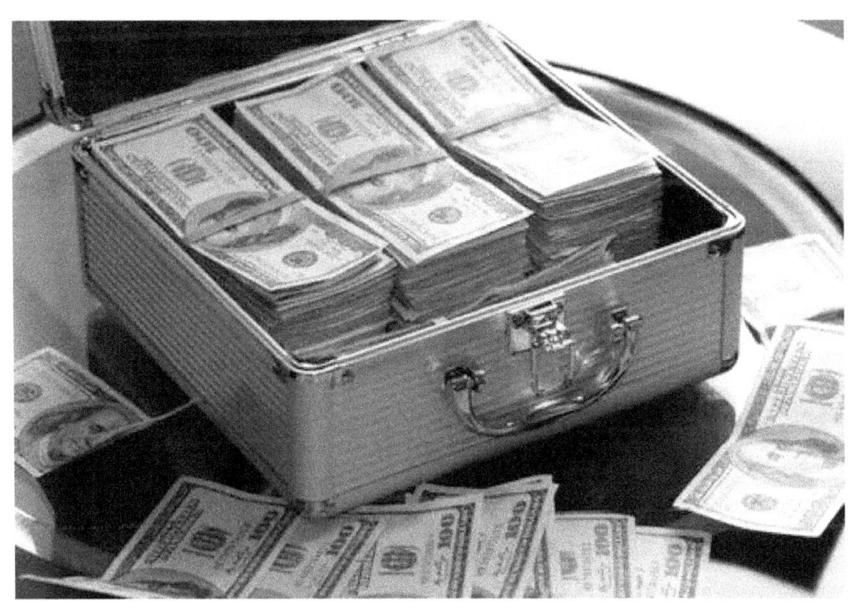

Chapter 4

Colossal Cash

from

Crowd Funding

Crowd Funding Crowd Sourcing

In 2015 over $34 billion dollars was raised by crowdfunding. Crowdfunding and Crowdsourcing roots began in 2005 and they help to finance or fund projects by raising money from a large number of people, usually by using the internet.

This type of fundraising or venture capital usually has 3 components. The individual or organization with a project that needs funding, groups of people who donate to the project, and a organization sets up a structure or rules to put the two together.

These websites do charge fees. The standard fee for success is about %5. If your goal is not met there is also a fee.

Below is a list of the top Crowdfunding websites according to myself and Entrepreneur Magazine Contributor Sally Outlaw.

Crowd Funding Crowd Sourcing

https://www.indiegogo.com/

Started as a platform for getting movies made, now helps to raise funds for any cause.

http://rockethub.com/

Started as a platform for the arts, now it helps to raise funds for business, science, social projects and education.

http://peerbackers.com/

Peerbackers focuses on raising funds for business, entrepreneurs and innovators.

https://www.kickstarter.com/

The most popular and well know n of all the crowdfunding websites. Kickstarter focuses on film, music, technology, gaming, design and the creative arts. Kickstarter only accepts projects from the United States, Canada and the United Kingdom.

Crowd Funding Crowd Sourcing

Group Growvc

http://group.growvc.com/

This website is for business and technology innovation.

https://microventures.com/

Get access to angel investors. This website is for business startups.

https://angel.co/

Another website for business startups.

https://circleup.com/

Circle up is for innovative consumer companies.

https://www.patreon.com/

If you start a YouTube Channel (highly recommended) you will hear about this website frequently. This website is for creative content people.

Crowd Funding Crowd Sourcing

https://www.crowdrise.com/

"Raise money for any cause that inspires you."
The Landing page slogan speaks for itself. #1
fundraising website for personal causes.

https://www.gofundme.com/

This fundraising website allows for business, charit
education, emergencies, sports, medical, memorial
animals, faith, family, newlyweds etc...

https://www.youcaring.com/

The leader in free fundraising. Over $400 million
raised.

https://fundrazr.com/

FundRazr is an award-winning online fundraising
platform that has helped thousands of people and
organizations raise money
for causes they care about.

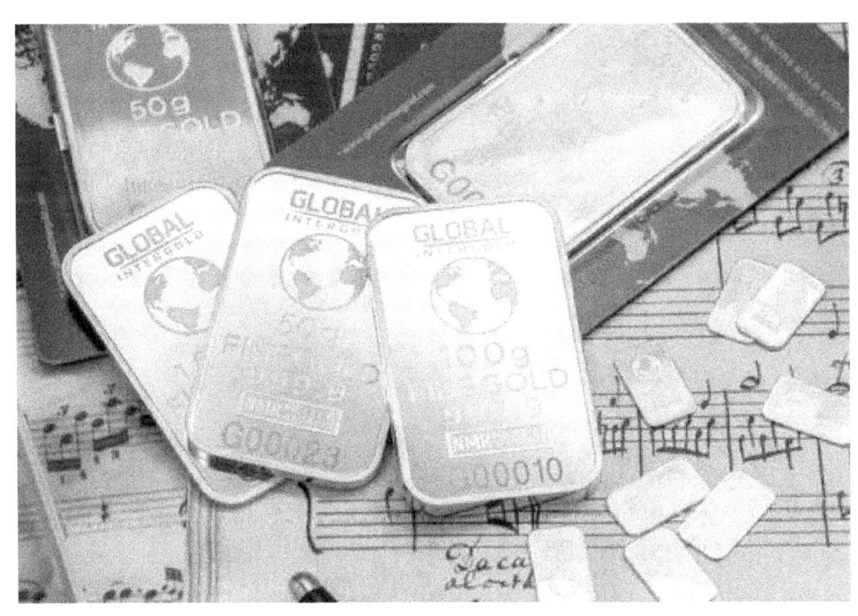

GLOBAL
INTERGOLD
50g
GOLD
GLOBAL
INTERGOLD
GLOBAL
INTERGOLD
100g
FINE GOLD
G00010
G00023

Chapter 5

$5 Million Government Dollars to Fund Your Business

$5 Million Dollars to Fund Your Business

Loans guaranteed by the Small Business Administration can be as little as $500 to as big as $5 Million Dollars!

The money can be used for a variety of business needs, including the purchase of long-term fixed assets and for operating expenses. Some loan programs do have restrictions on how the loan money can be used, so you will have to check with a Small Business Administration approved lender when looking for a loan. The lender can match you with the correct loan for your business needs.

Working Capital

Like seasonal financing, export loans, revolving credit, and refinanced business debt.

Fixed Assets

Like office equipment, property, tools, machinery, business equipment, construction, and remodeling.

$5 Million Dollars to Fund Your Business

Eligibility requirements

Lenders and loan programs have distinctive eligibility guide lines. Basically, eligibility is related to what a business does to receive its funding, the character of its ownership, and location of the businesses operation. Usually, businesses must meet size standards.

What is a small business size standard?

A size standard, under most circumstances is stated in number of employees or average yearly receipts, and represents the biggest size that a business (including its subsidiaries and affiliates) may be to remain classified as a small business for Small Business Administration and government contracting programs. The definition of "small" can be different in different industries.

How to calculate your small business size

Size standards are mostly based on the average annual receipts or the average number of employees

$5 Million Dollars to Fund Your Business

Eligibility requirements

 You must be able to repay the loan. You must have a credible business objective. Individuals with bad credit may still qualify for business startup money. Lenders will give you a list of the lending guide lines and requirements for your loan. Here are a few more.

Be a for-profit business

The business is properly registered and performs as a legal business.

Do business in the U.S.

The business is physically located and operates in the United States and or its territories.

You Have invested equity

You the business owner has invested your own time or finances into the business.

Eligibility requirements

Exhaust financing options

The business cannot get money from any other financial lender.

Loans for exporters

Most United States banks view loans for exporters a risky. This can make it more difficult for you to get loans for things like day-to-day operations, advance orders with suppliers, and debt refinancing. That's why the Small Business Administration came up wit programs to make it easier for United States small businesses to get loans for an export business.

To learn how the SBA can help you get an export loan, contact your local Small Business Administration International Trade Finance Specialis or the Small Business Administration's Office of International Trade.

https://www.sba.gov/funding-programs/loans

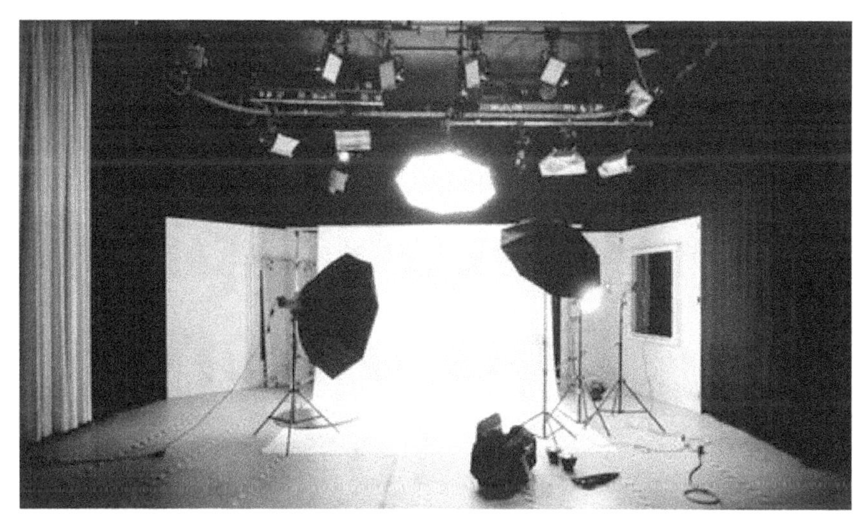

Chapter 6

Photography Equipment for Beginners

Photography Equipment for Beginners

Camera

A camera is the most important and expensive part of your photography equipment beginners kit. So for that reason: this is were we begin and this is where you will be given the most options.

The considerations for this list are price, camera size, functions and ease of use.

Canon Eos 200d (Rebel SL2)

24.2 effective megapixel APS-C CMOS sensor

DIGIC 7 image processor

Continuous Shooting Speed of 5 fps

ISO sensitivity 100-25600, expandable to 51200

9-point AF system, with centre point AF cross type

3-inch touch-screen monitor

Liveview Mode, 100% coverage

Pop-up flash

https://urlzs.com/Eym5s (Google shopping $549.00)

https://urlzs.com/cf2gw (Lotstosave $479.00)

Photography Equipment for Beginners

Nikon 1576 D5600

24MP CMOS sensor with no optical low pass filter (OLPF)

3.2" Fully Articulated touchscreen LCD with 1.04M dots

Full HD 1080p / 60fps movie mode with auto-focus while filming, mono sound, and stereo external mic support.

Active D-Lighting (four levels)

Eye-level pentamirror single-lens reflex viewfinder

Inbuilt time-lapse movie feature

2,016-pixel RGB sensor assists AF tracking and metering

'SnapBridge' Bluetooth/Wi-Fi communication

Built-in or external stereo microphone; sensitivity adjustable

https://urlzs.com/RvE4i (Google Shop $370-$390)

https://urlzs.com/fuBnF (Amazon Bundle $689.00)

Photography Equipment for Beginners

PANASONIC LUMIX DC-ZS70K

20. 3 Megapixel MOS sensor plus 30x Leica DC VARIO ELMAR lens (24 720mm)

Plus 5 axis Hybrid O. I. S. (Optical image Stabilizer)

0. 2 Inch 1, 166k dot EVF (electronic view finder) with eye sensor for easier viewing under sunny outdoor conditions

4K QFHD video recording (3840x2160)

Plus exclusive Lumix 4K PHOTO and 4K post focus with internal focus Stacking feature

Lens barrel mounted control ring enables quick, intuitive operation of important functions

Wi Fi plus a 180 Degree front Flip up touch feature enabled screen simplifies selfie photography, and framing for unusual perspectives.

Recording file format:Motion Picture: AVCHD Progressive, AVCHD

MP4.Wifi:IEEE 802.11b/g/n

https://urlzs.com/XUZfL (Amazon $347.99)

https://urlzs.com/SznCn (B&Hphotovideo $259.95)

Fujifilm X-T20

24.3 MGPX

More focus points

X-Trans CMOS III

X-Processor Pro image processor

Improved autofocus performance

4k video recording at 30 fps

Acros film simulation

A touchscreen with focus point selection

https://urlzs.com/fTFRx (BHPhotovideo $678.95)

https://www.adorama.com/ifjxt20bk1.html

(Adorama $799.00)

Photography Equipment for Beginners

Canon eos 800d (rebel t7i)

New 24.2-megapixel CMOS sensor with Dual Pixel CMOS AF

45 cross-type AF points

DIGIC 7, standard ISO 100–25600, H:51200

High-speed Continuous Shooting at up to 6.0 fps

Built-in Bluetooth.

1080p at 60/50 fps video recording capability

https://urlzs.com/VHoCR (Amazon $599.99)

https://urlzs.com/kX4ez (Walmart $579.90)

Photography Equipment for Beginners

Other Equipment needed:

1. Backdrop stands

2. Card Readers

3. Clamps

4. Lenses

5. Lights

6. Memory cards

7. Multi Disk Reflector

8. Octoadom photo flex

9. Photography Umbrella

10. Strobe Lights

11. Tripods

12. Universal speed ring

Photography Equipment for Beginners

1. Backdrop stands

Abs Photo's Video Backdrop Stand Kit 10 Tall x 12.3 Wide With Dual Air Cushion $ 83.31

10ft x 10ft Adjustable Heavy Duty Pipe and Drape Kit Backdrop Support with Weighted Steel Base $149.99

Aceexhibits FlexDrop Adjustable Backdrop Stand $ 440.00

2. Card Readers

Transcend USB 3.0 Multi Card Reader - White #TS-RDF8W $ 12.00

X1SMA6 Lexar Professional LRW400 Dual Slot SD & CF Reader $ 34.95

Kingston Technology USB 3.0 Hi-Speed Memory Card Media Reader Writer #FCR-HS4 $ 17.99

3. Clamps

Clamps are needed in photography for tightening up clothes, hanging backdrop to holding heavy equipment. Here are the types of clamps most used in photography.

"A" Clamps PJ Tool

Super Clamp

Cardellini Clamp http:// www.cardelliniclamp.com/

Platypus Clamp http:// www.hardwarefy.com

"C" Clamp

Photography Equipment for Beginners

4. Lenses

Sigma 17-50mm f/ 2.8 EX DC OS HSM Auto Focus Wide Angle Zoom Lens for Nikon Digital SLR Cameras $ 279.00

The Sigma 17-50mm is commonly used for Landscape/ scenery, Low light, Night photography, Sports/ action, Video, Weddings and more. The Sigma 17-50mm is most used by customers who consider themselves to be a Casual photographer, Photo enthusiast, Semi-pro photographer among others. The Sigma 17-50mm is popular because customers like the following qualities of the Sigma 17-50mm: Consistent output, Durable, Easily interchangeable, Fast / accurate auto-focus, Lightweight, Nice bokeh, Rugged and Strong construction.

Sigma 50mm f/ 1.4 DG HSM ART Lens for Sony Alpha & Maxxum DSLR Cameras Features $ 599.00

The Sigma 50mm F1.4 DG HSM Art is a pro-level performer for full-frame DSLRs and is ideal for many types of videography and photography, including portraits, landscapes, studio work and still-life. It has been redesigned and re-engineered with SLD glass and has been optimized for rich peripheral brightness, with improved large aperture performance by positioning wide elements into the front groups.

5. Lights

Docooler Portable Video Studio Photography Light Lamp Panel 176 LEDs 5600K for DSLR Camera ($ 24.99)

Designed with 176pcs LEDs, high brightness. Small size and light weight, very convenient for indoor and outdoor photography. It is an ideal companion for professional photographer and enthusiast. With 176pcs high-quality LED beads, output high brightness, 5600K color temperature.

Viltrox VL-162T Professional Bi-Color Dimmable LED Video Light $ 31.98

With Digital LCD Panel / 3300K-5600K 12W CRI 95 + / for Canon Nikon Sony DSLR Camera Camcorder Brand:

Aputure AL-M9 Amaran Pocket-Sized Daylight-Balanced LED Light $ 45.00

The Amaran AL-M9 is a LED fill light so small it fits in your pocket. It's compact and incedibly lightweight with 9 SMD bulbs that are powerful in the palm of your hand. It provides a max of 900lux that is able to do close-up fill light. You can use this light for a wide variety of applications to quick moving video to macro product photography, promising unlimited potential for how you can use this light.

6. 64GB Memory Cards

Transcend 64GB SDXC Ultimate Class 10 UHS-1 Memory Card, 90MB/ s Max Transfer Rate $ 40.99

https:// www.adorama.com/

Lexar 64GB Professional Class 10 UHS-I U1 633x SDXC Memory Card, Up to 95MB/ s Read, Up to 20MB/ $ 28.00

SanDisk Extreme PRO 64GB UHS-I Class 10 U3 V30 SDXC Memory Card $ 36.00

7. Multi Disk Reflector

110CM 43" 5-in-1 Photography Studio Multi Photo Disc Collapsible Light Reflector $20.88

Photoflex MultiDisc 5-in-1 Reflector (22") B&H # PHMD22 MFR # 870220

Google Express International Square Perfect Collapsible 43-Inch 5-in-1 Light Photo Disc Reflector (Set of 5) (2811 SP-43 5in1 Disc), Yellow Sunshine

Photography Equipment for Beginners

8. Octoadom photo flex

bhphotovideo.com

Photoflex Inner Diffusion Baffle for Medium OctoDome Softbox $ 17.95

9. Photography Umbrella

Cameta Camera Photoflex 45" Convertible White Satin Umbrella with Removable Black Cover Our Price: $ 39.95

Best Buy™ - 33" Dual-Layer Umbrella - White/ Silver/ Black $ 14.99

10. Strobe Lights

Westcott Strobelite, 150 Watt Second Monolight with 100 Watt Modeling Ligh $149.90

The Wescott Strobelight features 150 watt/second capability and a recycle time of 2 seconds at full power. Lightweight, durable and inexpensive, the Wescott Strobelight is an effective solution for studio shooting.

Dynalite Baja B4 Battery-Powered Monolight $ 599.00

Product Highlights 2.4 GHz Power Control Wireless Receiver 400Ws, 6-Stop Power Range 1/ 10 Stop Power Increments Rechargeable Li-Ion Battery Power

Dynalite Wireless Transmitter for Baja B4 Monolight $63.00

The Wireless Transmitter for Baja B4 Monolight from Dynalite allows wireless triggering of the Baja, as well as power level control at distances up to 590'. Operating on the 2.4 GHz frequency, the hot shoe style transmitter offers 6 separate groups with 16 channels and flash syncs as short as 1/ 250 sec. This transmitter will not give you High Speed Sync. To take advantage of HSS Canon users need to purchase a dedicated DYBRT616C Transmitter. Nikon users need to purchase a dedicated BYBRT616N Transmitter and also a DYBRR616N dedicated receiver to replace the one that comes with the Baja. Frequency 2.4 GHz Range 590' (180 m) Channels and Groups 16 Channels, 6 groups Flash Sync 1/ 250 Sec. Power 1x AA battery (included) Packaging Info Package Weight 0.35 Box Dimensions (HxWxD) 2.5 x 4.0 x 6.0

11. Tripod

Crutchfield.com

Nikon Prostaff Full Size Tripod $52.95

Walmart online

72" Pro Portable DV Video Camera Tripod Steady Stand Fluid Damping Head Kit w/ Bag 33lbs Capacity $ 104.95

Jet.com

72 In. Pro Portable Aluminum DV Video Camera Tripod Stand Fluid Pan Head Kit w/ Carrying Bag

12.   Universal speed ring

Newegg.com

Loadstone Studio Photography Softbox Universal Speed Ring For Photo Studio Lighting, NE_LI1067 $ 17.00

Walmart

Fotodiox Softbox Universal Speedring Speed Ring and Plate for Strobe Lights - Fits 3-6in Diameter Strobe Heads $ 19.95

Web sites to locate photography equipment:

efavormart.com

www.adorama.com/

BHPhotoVideo.com

Photography Equipment for Beginners

Camera Cleaning Kit

Many things like dust and moisture can damage camera bodies, lenses, and accessories. So you should protect your investment with a camera cleaning kit. The price of replacing or repairing your camera is negligable compared to the cost of a camera cleaning kit.

Camera Bag

Get a property designed camera bag to carry your photography equipment. You have invested to much in your equipment, not to have a quality bag to carry it in. It also shows you customers your commitment to quality. There are large DSLR gadget bags and backpack bags as an alternative.

Camera Strap

The difference in the quality of camera straps can be tremendous, so make sure you invest in a high quality camera strap to avoid your camera falling and incurring a costly repair.

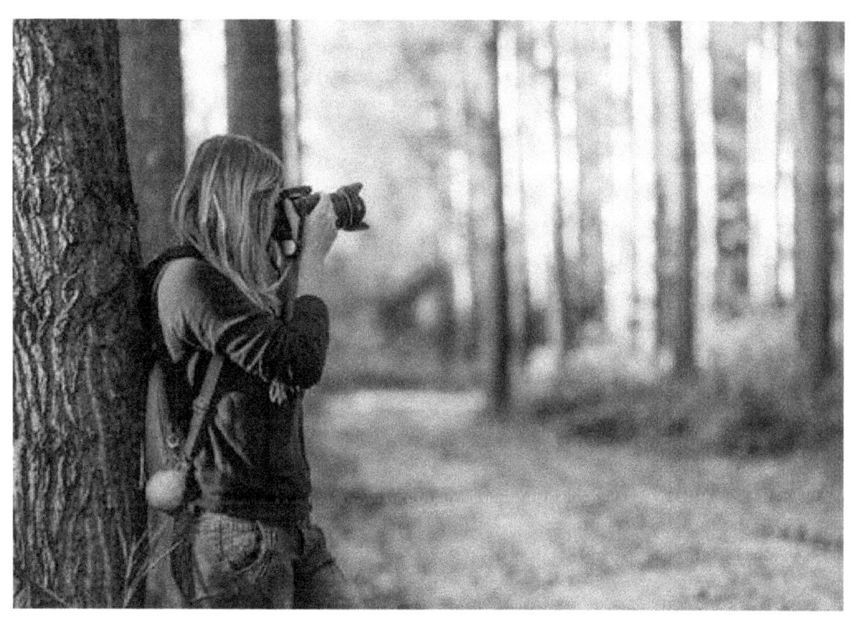

Chapter 7

Introduction to Freelancing

Introduction to Freelancing

A freelance worker is a person who seeks employment, usually on a temporary basis. Often time one short contract at a time. Sometimes a freelancer uses an agency that specializes in suppling labor for business clients or one could have their own business where work is bought to them. There are now plenty of websites that specialize in freelance work.

There are many industries that regularly use freelance workers: Writers, Web Developers, Computer Programmers, Editors, Music, Copywriters, Actors, translators, illustrators are some of the most popular fields, but the freelance industry can include many more occupations.

Introduction to Freelancing

Freelance Application

Resent statistics from a Freelance Industry so what Freelancers list as their Primary Skill:

20% Design

18% Writing

10% Editing

10% Copy writing

8%   Translating

5.5% Web Development

4%   Marketing

Over the years the freelance industry has changed. Many industries now require clients to sign contracts. A freelancer may require a deposit from a client, and may also be required to provide a documented estimate of the work, depending on the client. Some freelancers may still work for free on one project in order to get paid on another project. Each Freelance website has a different set of protocols for their freelancers and their clients.

Introduction to Freelancing

Freelance Payment

How do I get paid when I work freelance? How you get paid when you work freelance, depends on the industry that you work in. It depends on your skill level and your experience. It also depends on if you use a website to get your job or project. If you are getting your own jobs you can charge by the day, hour, rate or a per-project basis. You could also use a flat rate fee based on the market value of your work. Payment arrangements are made upfront and sometimes a percentage paid upfront is the custom, and the rest upon completion. More complex jobs may require a detailed contract with a payment schedule. One of risks of being a freelancer is that there is sometimes no guarantee of full payment.

Sometimes a writer or people in other artistic fields create work on their own and then seek a publisher for their work. They usually keep the copyright to the works and sell or license the rights to publishers in a time limited contract. Usually the work would be submitted to publishers as unsolicited query letters or manuscripts, and would get either a acceptance letter or rejection slip.

Introduction to Freelancing

When you a create intellectual property under a freelancer situation (according to the publishers' or other customers' specifications) are sometimes referred to as "independent contractors" or other similar terms.

Section 101 of the U.S. Copyright Act of 1976 (17 USC §101). Details "works made for hire", protection of intellectual property is defined.

Demographics

A new era has begun. Nine to five has defined what many people traditionally think of as a job.

Times are quickly changing. Over 53 million Americans are now earning income from jobs that are considered freelance or independent contracting. That is %33 percent of the United States workforce.

The current increase in freelance work is similar the the Industrial Revolution of times past.

The surge in freelancing is more than two decades old at this point.

The freelancing increase began over twenty years ago, when with the increase in technology many more people were able to work from project to project. It was about that time that the Freelancers Union was formed by Sarah Horowitz.

Introduction to Freelancing

About 70% of the Freelance industry is made up of women between the ages of 30 to 50. So while the regular journalism field is made up predominately of men, the freelance writing profession is mainly women.

Benefits

Freelancers have many of reasons for freelancing, the profit gained differ by gender, industry, and way of life. Recently Freelance Industry Report reported that males and females do freelance work for different reasons. Women in the survey said that they prefer the scheduling freedom and flexibility that freelancing offers, while men in the survey said they freelance to follow or pursue personal goals.

Freelancing helps people to obtain greater levels of employment in isolated communities.

Workers who have been laid-off have decided to be freelancers because they can't find full-time jobs for some industries like the newspaper industrie which has been declining recently. Students have become freelancers using some of their free time during the school year. Flexibility is always rated high on blogs and in interviews on websites.

Introduction to Freelancing

Drawbacks

Their are plenty of websites that specialize in Freelance work and offer plenty of advice and work for freelancers.

Freelancers usually live without job security. They also have to deal with employers who don't pay on time. Freelancers usually don't have employment benefits such as pension, sick leave, paid holidays, bonuses or health insurance.

Answers to Drawbacks

The use of freelance websites can usually eliminate the problems with payments.

Using multiple freelance websites can stockpile tons of work to add to job security.

Because you are a freelancer and your own boss, you can give yourself sick leave and paid holiday.

Impact of the Internet

The power of the Internet has given the freelancer many more job oppurtunities. There are growing markets for writers, editors, illustrators, graphic design, computer programmer, web developers, photographers and many more rising jobs.

Introduction to Freelancing

Recent stories on CNBC and other news outlets show that online outsourcing and crowdsourcing are becoming more popular with many of the top websites like Upwork and Toptal with over a million clients. More companies are leveraging technology to fill labor shortages. Many compainies are even going outside of the United States for computer freelance work. Micro Work Sites like fiverr have become very popular.

This book will show you plenty of the top freelance websites and online marketplaces that match workers and clients using the internet. Most sites use a bidding service, fixed price or an hourly rate. Workers get paid through a merchant account supervised by the website. The website makes money by getting small percentage of each transaction.

With the internet the interview process and hiring for freelancers can be done without actually seeing the employer in person. This is amazing for being able to do long distance work all over the world. There is a drawback, because the screening process is less personal.

Introduction to Freelancing

But the internet allows you to hire more than one person and test out their work. Fiverr is an exellent website to "test out talent" before committing to a big job. Especially for writing. With the explosion of the Amazon Kindle, many people are looking for internet writers to assist in creating content for books. Many need photographers to assist with book covers. With more and more blogs and webpages being put up, the demand for information technology continues to increase.

It is estimated that Amazon holds %67 of the online publishing business and %25 to Barnes and Noble. Amazon recently reported that their online electronic books have surpassed and even doubled the sales of their print books. So the need for writers has really exploded with the use of the Internet. The use of the internet and the Amazon explosion has also resulted in an increase in copy editing of book and book manuscripts and proofreading services being outsourced to freelance copy editors and proofreaders.

There are many top freelancer websites. We will go into detail about the top freelancer websites in another chapter.

Introduction to Freelancing

A few Legal aspects

For legal advice in your business consult the appropriate professional.

Some newspapers allow a writer the option of ghost signing. That is when a writer does not use their name in the byline of their article. Ghost signing allows a writer to get benefits while still being classified as a freelancer. While ghost signing is a big issue in the UK(IR35 violations) it does not matter much in the United States.

Freelancers have to handle promotion, contracts, law issues and finance and business responsibilities by themselves.

Freelancers run the risk of losing too much of their profit and have to be careful of expenses when using other professionals in their business.

The United States Federal government in 2009 began to increase their montering of freelancers and other independent contractors.

The (GAO) United States Government Accountability Office instructed the Secretary of Labor to look at freelancers or independent contractors during targeted investigations. Their targeting involves appropriate employment taxes and unemployment and workers compensation.

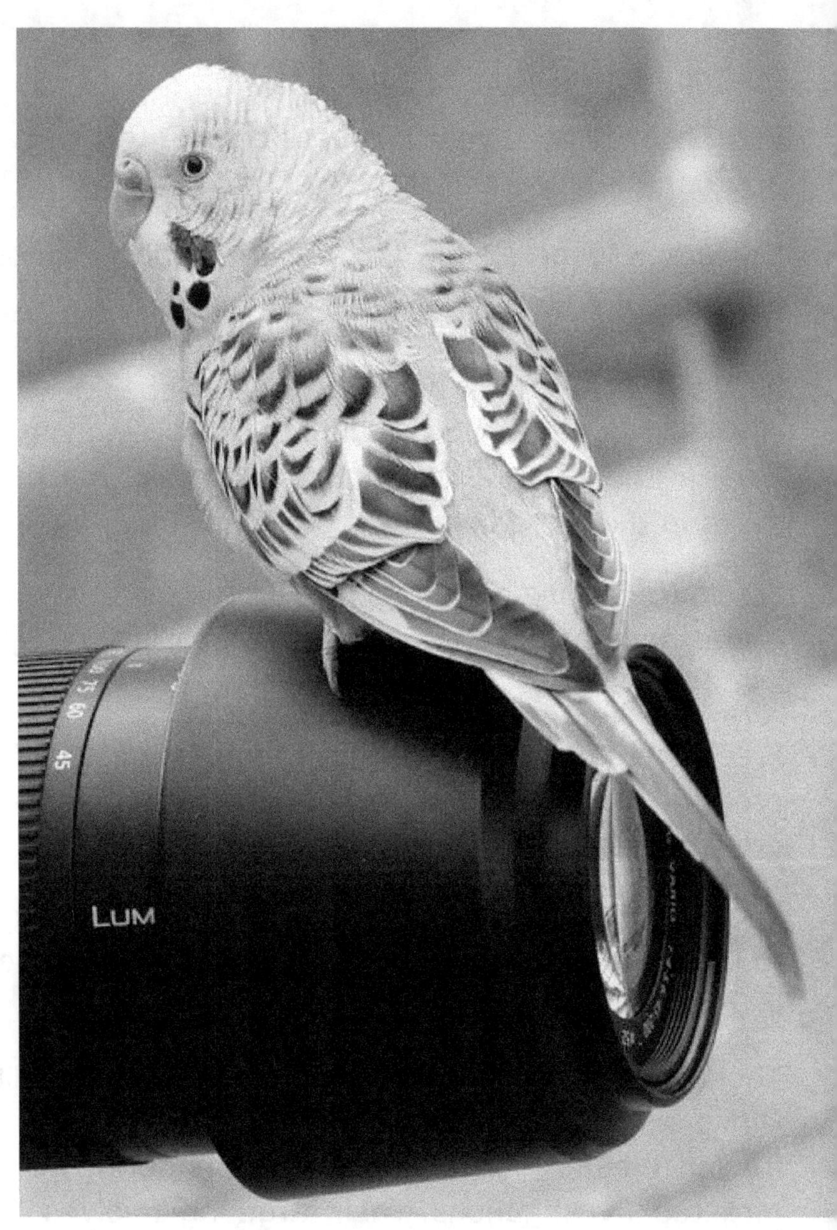

LUM

Chapter 8

The Best Job Freelancing Web Sites

The Best Job Freelancing Sites

1. Upwork

With over 1.5 million clients and over 9 million registered users **Upwork** (formerly oDesk) likely ha something for you regardless of where you are in your career. Upworkd is good for small and big projects. Upwork has hourly projects as well as per project gigs. There are jobs for experts as well as entry level. This is the largest freelancing website o the market.

Because of the massive size of this website, many o the jobs have a lot of competition which leads to lo bid contests. The site also has fixed bids as well. It a good strategy to lower your usual rate to get som jobs and build up a good reputation and rating on t site.

2. Toptal

*Unparalleled access to meaningful projects with great clients and fair compensation.

Toptal is more for freelancers with experience. Topt has a screening process you have to pass and whicl leads to high level fortune 500 clients. The compensation is fair with no low bid contests. Topta also has frequent meetups and tech events.

The Best Job Freelancing Sites

This website has been constructed for top of the line software engineers that must pass a difficult screening process. Toptal is looking for people with experience, good communication skills as well as a high level of technical know how. Toptal offers a risk free trial period. Once accepted you can set your own hourly rates.

3. Elance

As of the printing of this book (2016), the Elance website is still up, but it has merged with Upwork.

4. Freelancer

Freelancer is a big platform with lots of clients. In addition to offering millions of projects, freelancer allows you to compete with other freelancers in contests to prove your skills, showcase your abilities, and attract more clients.

If you are just starting out, because of the contests, and the large number of competitors might make this a website to try later on in your career.

The Best Job Freelancing Sites

5. Craigslist

Craigslist is more than just a website to buy and sell household products and personal belongings. It is also a great source for freelance jobs. You can easily browse local offerings or you can search by major cities if you prefer working remotely.

While Craigslist is not a freelance only jobsite it's size makes it a great cost effective place to find freelance jobs.

6. Guru

Easily showcase your past work experience and use the daily job-matching feature to avoid missing any good opportunities.

Guru has a work room designed to let you manage all of your work, quickly and easily.

At first Guru focused on the United States, but now Guru is global website that is constanly expanding.

Guru primarily deals with computer programming coding but other professions are represented as well

The Best Job Freelancing Sites

Guru has great project tracking features but also has high fees and a challenging withdrawal system, that you could incur more fees. Particularly with smaller jobs.

7. 99designs

This is a great website for freelance designers. 99designs allows you to compete in design contests and get feedback as clients choose the best ones. A great way for talented designers to prove their skills. Be careful to protect yourself from plagiarism when using this website.

8. Peopleperhour

Peopleperhour A great platform, focusing on freelancing for web projects. If you're a designer, developer, SEO specialist, etc., This site is worth checking out.

This website can have high fees and challenging customer service support.

The Best Job Freelancing Sites

9. Freelance Writing Gigs

Freelance Writing Gigs. The name almost says it all. This is a website for publishers, writers, editors, bloggers or any one who has talent with words.

10. Demand Media

Demand Media is a website for creative types to promote their talent, including writers, filmmakers, producers, **photographers**, and more.

This a a great website For Clients that need these types of creative people.

11. College Recruiter

The college student or recent graduate, often is faced with the dilemma of not having experience when searching for a job. Well, the College Recruiter website is for college students or recent graduates looking for freelance jobs of any type.

College Recruiter is a great place to get a jump on your career or earn some money doing part time work.

The Best Job Freelancing Sites

This is a website usually for smaller projects that can be done by people that do not have a lot of experience.

12. GetACoder

GetACoder is a freelancing website that focuses primarily on small projects for computer programmers, writers, web developers. This is an excellent website for freelancers that don't want to be loaded up with long term (three to six month) projects.

13. iFreelance

Unlike other sites, iFreelance is a freelancer website that allows you to keep 100% of your earnings. It accomodates writers, editors, coders, and even freelance marketers.

The Best Job Freelancing Sites

14. Project4hire

Project4hire has a ton of job categories. Easily identify jobs that suit your skillset with hundreds of project categories to choose from.

This website is primarily for computer programmers, consultants and designers. Although there are jobs for other professions.

15. SimplyHired

SimplyHired is a freelance website that is not focused on tech but has a wider range of jobs than most. This site is perfect for anyone from salespeople to construction workers.

SimplyHired has a blog with hiring tips, a company directory and location-based search. This is the perfect website for people whose skillset is not technology based.

The Best Job Freelancing Sites

16. Staff.com

Staff.com is a freelance website that is primarily for long term freelancers. Staff.com is smaller that some of the other websites in this list and gives freelancers looking for more stable work a place to go to.

17. LinkedIn

LinkedIn is a well known professional network. It features a large collectiong of resumes and professional profiles. There are many options on this website to help you increase your exposure for professional work. There are also professional courses to help you to maximize the many features on this website.

18. StackExchange

StackExchange is not a website that is dedicated to freelance workers. It does have a extremly popular Questian and Answer forum that can be used to connect with freelance or independent contractors and employers. It could take more work than other websites, but is still a place were a freelancer can network to get a job.

The Best Job Freelancing Sites

19. Jobs.smashingmagazine.com

An excellent portal for developers and designers to find freelance jobs.

20. FLEXJOBS.COM

This freelance website stands out by vetting jobs, no freelancers. In return, flexjobs provides a job list of just under 30,000 projects with contact information.

Whether you are a computer programmer, web designer, experienced, or just out of college or something in between, there is a freelance platform out there for you.

This website also has skill testing and job search tips

PHOTOGRAPHY

21. Journalism.com

Open an account on the website and then use photography queries to narrow the search results.

22. freelancephotographerjobs.com

Photographer Jobs is the United States, Canada and the United Kingdom.

The Best Job Freelancing Sites

23. photography-jobs.net

Upload photos and instantly sell to millions of potential buyers.

Receive payments via paypal, wire transfer or mailed checks.

Turn a hobby into a profitable business

24. journalismjobs.com

Just type Photographer into the search box and jobs with good descriptions come up on the landing page.

25. virtualvocations.com/jobs

Virtual Vocations is a job service that provides job-seekers with hand-screened telecommuting jobs leads that offer real pay for real work. From account management to writing, all of the job openings we bring you offer some form of telecommuting or virtual work.

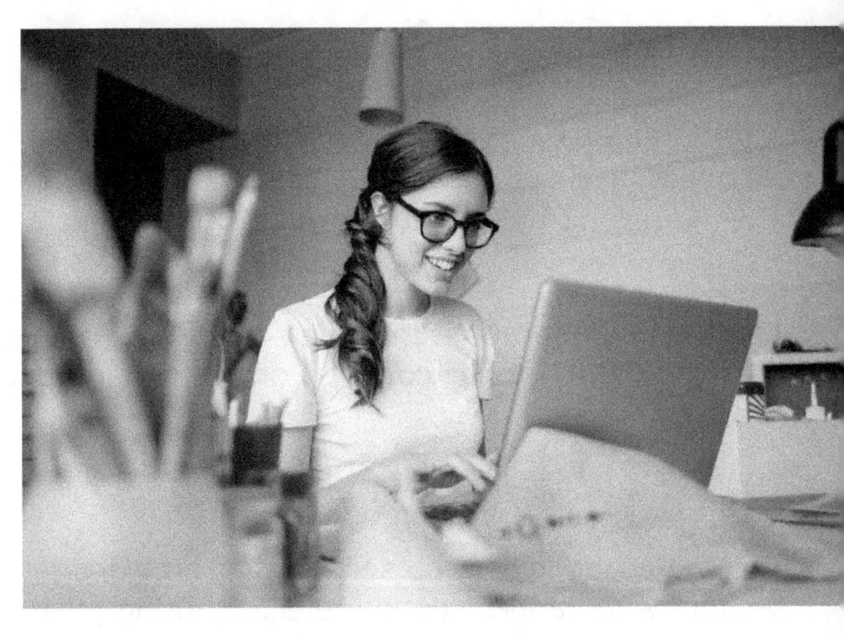

Chapter 9

Reach a Billion People
Video Marketing

YouTube Video Marketing Overview

Million Dollar Video Marketing

When you read the title of this book you may have thought the term "Million Dollar" was hyperbole. However the beauty of video marketing is that it ca be done for free, and that there really are several people who make millions of dollars just on their YouTube video's alone. Meaning that they allow ads to be placed on them and they get paid a portion of what google gets from businesses that runs the ads

Since they are only getting a portion of what is bein paid, that means if they make a million dollars, the video's actually produced multi-millions of dollars in ad revenue.

Here are a list of YouTube Millionaires as reported b Forbes magazine in the 20 December 2016 issue.

Youtube name/channel	2016 Income
1. Pewdiepie	$15 Million

Makes video's of himself playing video games and making crude comments on girls dancing.

| 2. Atwood | $8 Million |

YouTube Video Marketing Overview

Promotes products and tours with other Youtubers.

   3. Lilly Singh $7.5 Million

Makes comedy skits mostly featuring herself talking about her parents and relationship issues.

YouTube name/channel	2016 Income
4. Smosh	$7 Million
Comedy Duo.	
5. Rosanna Pasino Nerdie Nummies	$6 Million
Baking show	
6. Markipler	$5.5 Million
Comments on Video Games.	
7. German Garmendia	$5.5 Million
Got a publishing deal from his YouTube channel	
8. Miranda Sings	$5 Million
Comedian	

YouTube Video Marketing Overview

9. Collen Ballinger $5 Million

Comedian

10. Tyler Oakley $5 Million

Makes a diary. LGBT Activist

And these are just some the the top earners. There are many more making $50,000 a month talking about movies, how to put on make up or video taping a day at an amusement park.

A Few Keys to Video Marketing Success

1. Commitment

While many of the top YouTubers are funny, they take their business seriously. One of the first things you have to understand is that there is commitment needed to be successful on YouTube.

Many of the successful YouTubers put up video's daily! One such YouTuber is Grace Randolph (Beyond the Trailer). Grace comments on movie news and movie trailers. She typically uploads 3 video's a day.

YouTube Video Marketing Overview

2. Research

Just putting up a video will not guarantee views. You have to put in research for every video. Research if the topic is popular or trending. Research what keywords you should use in your video. Research the success of other video's. Skip the research, skip the success.

3. Popularity

There are certain topics on YouTube that are extremely popular. Star Wars, Disney, Scantily clad women, video games, comedy. Know the level of your topics popularity and try to use keyword planning to max out the highest possible level. Some educational material is extremely valuable, but not popular.

ZERO COST MARKETING OVERVIEW

This is a zero cost online marketing plan for any business, cause or idea you wish to promote. This plan will show you step by step how to use online marketing featuring YouTube and Article Marketing to get free advertising for this or any product. In addition, this report will show you how to use this zero cost marketing plan to create a passive income stream.

YouTube Video Marketing Overview

A Few Key Definitions

YouTube is a video-sharing website headquartered in San Bruno, California, United States. The service was created by three former PayPal employee in February 2005. In November 2006, it was bought by Google for 1.65 Billion dollars. According to the Huffington Post, YouTube has 1 billion active users each month. Or nearly one out of every two people on the internet.

AdSense (Google AdSense) is an advertising placement service by Google. The program is designed for website publishers who want to display targeted text, video or image advertisement on website pages and earn money when the site visitors view or click the ads.

Hyperlink is a link from a hypertext file or document to another location or file, typically activated by clicking on a highlighted word or image on the screen.

Black Hat

In search engine optimization (SEO) terminology, black hat SEO refers to the use of aggressive SEO strategies, techniques and tactics that focus only on search engines and not a human audience, and usually does not obey search engines guidelines.

YouTube Video Marketing Overview

Getting Started

You get started by opening up a YouTube account. Go to www.YouTube.com and follow the step by step instructions. Then you open up a AdSense account. The AdSense account will take about a week to open. AdSense is linked to your YouTube account and land bank account. AdSense will use your 9 digit routing number to deposit a small amount of money into your land bank account. You then have to report to AdSense the amount deposited. After the deposit is confirmed, AdSense will send you a postcard to verify your address. You must then report to AdSense the pin number locate on the postcard. Once all the verification takes place YouTube allows you to connect all of the accounts and by doing so, you can now monetize your video's and create a passive income stream.

Social Media

You should join Social Media web sites like Facebook, Google Plus, Digg, Twitter, Linkedin, Tumbler and Pinterest. Every time you upload a video. When you are finished Optimizing it, you should link it to all of your social media web sites. This creates Backlinks. A Backlink is an incoming hyperlink from one webpage to another. Google and YouTube will rank your video higher if it has a good number of Backlinks. However if you have too many, and it appears that you have created them artificially, then Google and YouTube can punish you by removing your video.

YouTube Video Marketing Overview

As long as you are backlinking organically and not using Black Hat software or Black Hat web sites, yo should be find with Google and YouTube.

Show Me the Money!

Monetization involves you allowing AdSense to plac ads that run before or are placed on your videos. If the ads are clicked on, you make money. If the ads are viewed in their entirety you make money.

After you have your accounts set up, you need to gather all of the tools you will be using to create videos. You can create your videos using a standard video camera and tripod and videotape yourself. Or any other number of ways you can capture video. However for this program we are going "zero cost" there will be no need to purchase or obtain a video camera.

Getting Free Tools to Create Your Videos

We are going to use "Screen Capture" software. Go to http://screencast-o-matic.com/home to downloa a free screen capture software called Screencast-o-Matic. There are two versions. The Free version allows you to videotape up to 15 minutes of conten and places a watermark on all of your recordings. The pro version makes longer recordings and has edit tools and not watermark. The pro version cost $15 and year and may be worth the investment on your business begins to make a profit.

YouTube Video Marketing
Overview

Then next tool you will use in creating your videos is a free copy of the office software package called Apache OpenOffice. Go to https://www.openoffice.org/download/ to download the software.

100% Copyright Free Content

Now that you have to tools to create a video, you need content. Wikipedia is an excellent source of copyright free content, you can use to create your videos. There are many keyword phrases that you can use to find material. Later on in this book you will learn how to use the Google Ad Planner to get the best keyword phrases to use in your videos.

YouTube Video Marketing
SEO – The Key to Internet Riches

Search Engine Optimization

Analytics: Video Viewership

Through out this book I am going to discuss many YouTube analytics that factor into how your video is ranked in YouTube. Once someone clicks onto your video to view it, YouTube keeps track of how many minutes it was view. Videos that are viewed from beginning to end get ranked higher base on the belie that the content is good if the viewer keeps watching it. For this reason, it is usually a good idea to keep most your videos under five minutes. It addition, this allows you to create more videos to a related topic. I is better to have twenty 3 minute videos than one 1 hour video, because it is more likely that the 3 minute videos will be watched in their entirety. Also by creating 20 videos you now have 20 possible places for AdSense to place monetized ads and thus increase your earning potential 20 times.

Tags, Keywords and Keyword Phrases

Tags, keywords and keyword phrases are the most important part of getting your YouTube video to rank on the first page of YouTube. There is an old saying..."If you commit murder, where do you hide the body, where nobody will find it? On the second page of Google".

YouTube Video Marketing SEO – The Key to Internet Riches

Although we are working on YouTube the principle is the same. You must rank on the first page of YouTube in order for your video to get views from standard YouTube web site traffic.

Keywords are words that relate to your video. Some keywords for business are:

Business, Marketing and Start-up

Keyword Phrases for business are:

how to make money from home, internet marketing, small business grants

Tags are Keywords or Keyword Phrases that you place on your YouTube video's editing page, in order to get viewers to find your video.

Your goal is to try to rank in the top 20(land on the first page of YouTube) for every or most of the Tags in your video.

Your Video Title

The title of your video should be a keyword phrase that you want to rank for. It should also be relevant to the content in the video. When your title, tags and description are all relevant it boosts your YouTube rankings.

YouTube Video Marketing
SEO – The Key to Internet Riches

Video Description

Each video is allowed to have a description. At the top of the description box, is where you should place a clickable or hyperlink, to either your web site or another video that you wish to viewer to see. Below the link should be a description of the video that contains content that is relative to the video. One short cut you can use it to cut and paste your video script into the description.

You video description should also have the keywords you used as tags. This adds to the videos relevancy.

You should also put links in you video to your social media addresses.

Half Time Adjustments

Any tags that are ranking your video in the top 20 should be placed in the headline/title of the video to boost their rank even higher.

One software that helps save you a tremendous amount of time doing this is called Tube Buddy.

https://www.tubebuddy.com/

YouTube Video Marketing
Writing Your Script

CREATING CONTENT

You have two options for creating content. On screen video of yourself using a digital camera or phone camera. Take notes of what you will discuss.

Know your topic before you hit record.

Recording Tips:

* Use good lighting.

* Try recording near a window during the day time.

* Limit background noise as much as possible.

* Use a POWERPOINT screen capture style video.

* Create bullet points

* Use free software like jing or camstudio to record it. You can also get a free 30 day trial of camtasia from TechSmith

* www.screencast-o-matic.com is another free solution.

* Use your computer's built in microphone.

YouTube Video Marketing
Writing Your Script

* Use a usb microphone is ideal, but not required.

* if you or kids have a usb gaming headset that works as well.

* most smart phones have a mp3 recording option.

Writing Your Script

Try to use words in your script that get and hold you
viewers attention. Words like... you, want, now, free
limited time, All-American, imagine and how to, are
just a few of the many words that are proven to stir
a viewers emotions. Viewing a few copy writing
videos on YouTube should help you to chose attentio
grabbing words.

AIDA is an acronym used in marketing and
advertising that describes a common list of events
that may occur when a consumer engages with an
advertisement.

- A – attention (awareness): attract the attention of the customer.
- I – interest of the customer.
- D – desire: convince customers that the want and desire the product or service and th it will satisfy their needs.
- A – action: lead customers towards taking action and/or purchasing.

YouTube Video Marketing
Writing Your Script

Using a system like this gives one a general understanding of how to target a market effectively. Moving from step to step, one loses some percent of prospects.

AIDA is a historical model, rather than representing current thinking in the methods of advertising effectiveness.

A basic rule of thumb for writing your script is that one paragraph equals about 60 seconds of talking. So if you are trying to shoot a 3 minute video you what to create a 3 paragraph document for your script. Try to use words in our script that are relevant to the title of your video.

You can also cut and paste your script into a YouTube video editor, and make your video Closed Captioned. This wIll increase your rankings in the YouTube search engine and it will allow more people to understand your video and increase your views.

CREATING TOPICS FOR YOUR VIDEOS

It is time to brainstorm and write down topics for your videos.

Remember you could choose a video around your own information product if you had it.

YouTube Video Marketing
Writing Your Script

Get a notepad and think of 10 to 20 FAQ about your business.

http://answers.yahoo.com

Is a good source to find out what the potiential customers of your business are interested in.

Also look at articles on ezinearticles.com and see what topics come up the most for articles related to your business.

You can also browse forums related to your business

Take a look at information products about your target market.

When you make a video that features Frequently Asked Questions each faq could be a short 1 to 3 minute video.

Use nichesuggest.com for a list of possible keyword ideas as well as seocentro and the google keyword planner.

Brainstorm 5 to 10 additional solution oriented videos. You should cover why the solution you are offering is better and why does your product recommendation solve your customer's problem.

YouTube Video Marketing
Writing Your Script

Try to think of every advantage possible. Read other reviews of similar products or businesses or view sales pages for ideas of content for your videos.

Creating a Multipurpose Close

There are certain things that you should say in almost all of your videos:

* Thank the viewer for watching

* Ask the viewer to Thumbs up or Like your video

* Ask the viewer to subscribe to your YouTube Channel

* Ask the viewer to leave a comment

* Ask the viewer to share your video link with friends or social media

YouTube Video Marketing
Writing Your Script

YOUR CALL TO ACTION

send your website visitors to a variety of places.

* A free website through weebly.com

* A free page through squidoo.com

* A free blog through blogspot.com

Use a tracking link like www.bit.ly or www.tinyurl.com

be careful as these links can change on you.

UPLOADING VIDEO

Create your account at www.youtube.com you can use a google account if you have one already created. Upload your video. Then provide your keyword rich video title. Look at other examples of videos performing well in that space. Use keywords from your niche or business and topic research write a good description with the keywords in it.

Try to include at least 2 sentences in your description. More content in your description will not hurt you. Include your website link at the beginning of the description use format http://www.yourfreelink.com encourage likes, comments, or honest feedback at the end of the description. Make a call to action in the description as well.

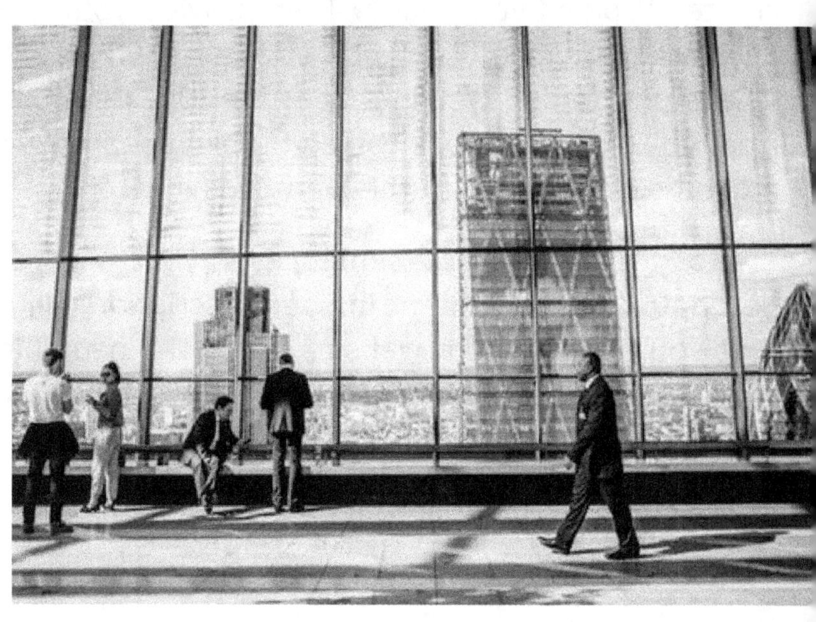

CHAPTER 10
Business Insurance

BUSINESS INSURANCE

Consult an attorney for any and all of your business matters.

In the early 1990's an elderly woman purchased a hot cup of coffee from a McDonald's drive-thru window in Albuquerque. She spilled the coffee, and suffered 3rd degree burns. She sued Mcdonald's and won. She won 2.7 million dollars in a punitive damages victory. The verdict was appealed and settlement is estimated at somewhere in the neighborhood of $500,000 dollars. All because she spilled the coffee into her lap, while trying to add sugar and cream.

Two men in Ohio, were carpet layers. They were severely burned when a three and a half gallon container of carpet adhesive ignited, when the hot water heater it was sitting next to, was turned on. They felt the warning lable on the back of the can was insufficient. So they filed a lawsuit against the adhesive manufacturers and were awarded nine million dollars.

A woman in Oklahoma, purchased a brand new Winnebago. While driving it home, she set the cruise control to 70 miles per hour. She then left the drivers seat to make some coffee or a sandwich in the back of the motor home.

BUSINESS INSURANCE

The vehicle crashed and the woman sued Winnebago for not advising her, that cruise control does not drive and steer the vehicle. She won 1.7 million dollars and the company had to rewrite their instruction manual.

Unfortunately all three outrageous lawsuits are real. If you are going to run a business, any business, you should consider protecting yourself with Professional Liability Insurance, also known as Errors and Omissions (E & 0) insurance.

This type of insurance can help to protect you from having to pay the full cost of defending yourself against a negligence lawsuit claim.

Error and Omissions can protect you against claims that are not usually covered in regular liability insurance. Those policies usually cover bodily harm, or damage to property. Error and Omissions can protect you agaist negligence, and other mental anguish like inaccurate advice, or misrepresentation. Criminal prosecution is not covered.

Errors and Ommision insurance is recommended for notaries public, real estate brokers or investors and professionals like: software engineers, lawyers, home inspectors web site delvelopers and landscape architects to name a few professions.

BUSINESS INSURANCE

The Most Common Errors and Omission Claims:

%25 Breach of Fiduciary Duty

%15 Breach of Contract

%14 Negligence

%13 Failure to Supervise

%11 Unsuitability

%10 Other

BUSINESS INSURANCE

Things you should know about or require before purchasing a Errors and Omission policy is...

* What is the limit of liability

* What is the Deductible

* Does it include FDD First Dollar Defense - which obligates the insurance company to fight a case without a deductible first.

* Do I have Tail-end coverage or Extended Reporting Coverage (insurance that lasts into retirement)

* Extended coverage for Employees

* Cyber Liability Coverage

* Department of Labor Fiduciary Coverage

* Insolvency Coverage

If you get Errors and Omission insurance, renew it the day it expires. You must be careful to avoid gaps in your coverage, or it could result in not getting your policy renewed.

BUSINESS INSURANCE

A few E & O Insurance Providers:

Insureon

Insureon states that their median Errors and Omissions Insurance policy cost about $750 a year about $65 a month. The price of course will vary according to your business, the policy you choose and other risk factors.

https://www.insureon.com/home

EOforless

EOforless.com helps insurance, investment, and real estate professionals buy E & O insurance at an affordable cost in five minutes or less.

https://www.eoforless.com/

BUSINESS INSURANCE

CalSurance Associates

As a leading insurance broker, CalSurance Associates, a division of Brown & Brown Program Insurance Services, Inc. has over fifty years of experience delivering comprehensive insurance products, exceptional service, and proven results to over 150,000 insured. They provide professionals nationwide and across multiple industries, including some of the largest financial firms and insurance companies in the United States.

http://www.calsurance.com/csweb/index.aspx

Better Safe Than Sorry

Insurance is one of the hidden costs of doing business. These are just a few companies and a brief overview on the topic of business insurance. Make sure to talk to an attorney or quailified insurance agent before making any decision on insurance. Protect you and your business. Many states do not require E & O insurances. But when you see the cost of some of the settlements, it's better to be safe than sorry.

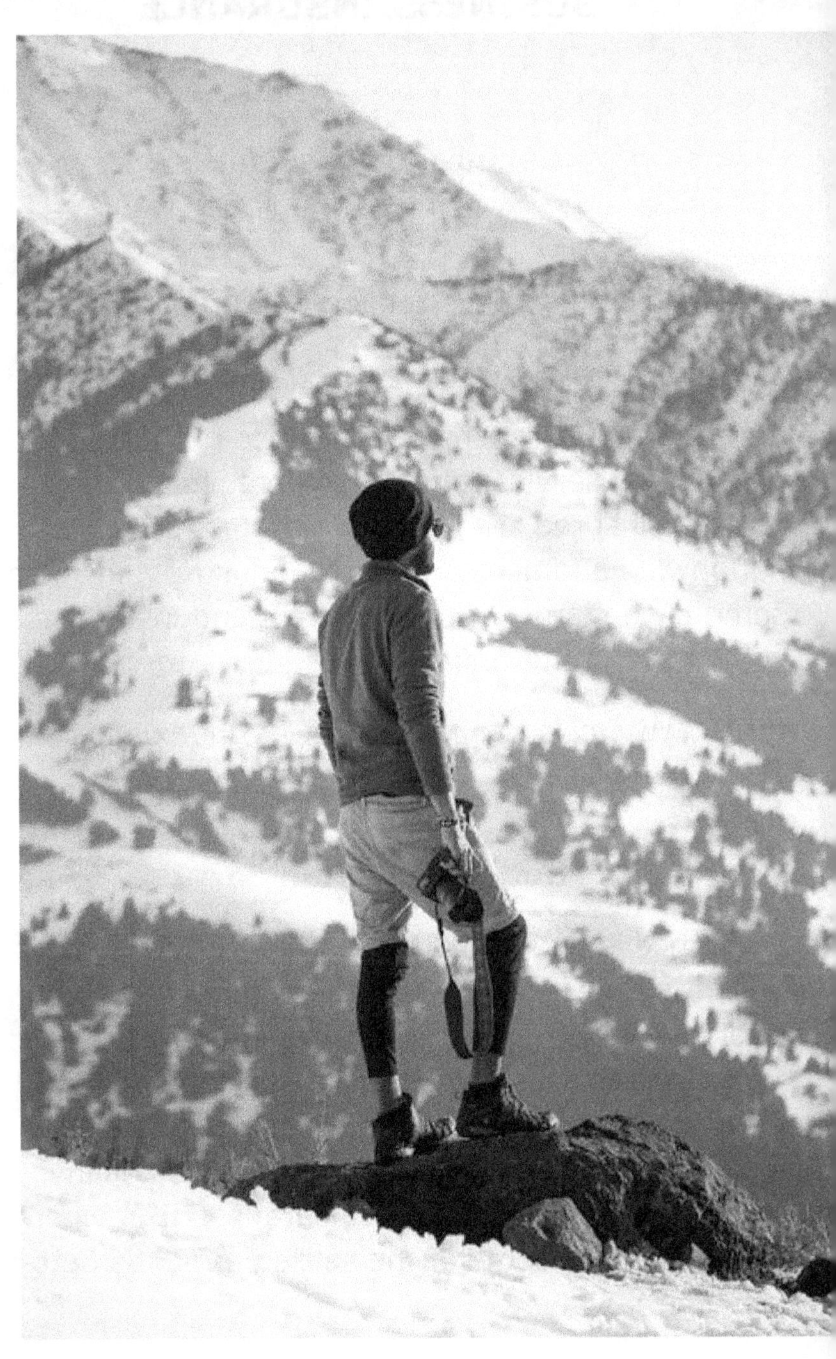

Chapter 11

Photography Business Web Site Resources

Web Site Resources

Free Information Creation Tools

You can download open office for free

https://www.**openoffice**.org/**download**

To create slides, ebooks, reports and PDF files.

You can download ScreenCast-o-Matic for free to create screen captor videos

https://screencast-o-matic.com/screen_recorder

Web Site Resources

Always ready Free Web Hosting Sites

www.weebly.com

www.wix.com

www.about.me

Automatic Alerts

www.google.com/alerts

www.talkwalker.com/

Top Freelancing Job Sites

https://www.Upwork.com

https://www.TopTal.COM

https://www.Jobs.smashingmagazine.com

https://www.Freelancer.com

https://www.Craigslist.com

https://www.Guru.com

https://www.99designs.com

https://www.PeoplePerHour.com

Web Site Resources

Top Freelancing Job Sites

https://www.Freelancewritinggigs.com

https://www.Demandmedia.com

https://www.Collegerecruiter.com

https://www.Flexjobs.com

https://www.Ifreelance.com

https://www.Project4hire.com

https://www.Simplyhired.com

https://www.staff.com

MICRO JOB SITES

https://www.fiverr.com/

https://www.fourerr.com

https://www.seoclerks.com

http://www.clickchores.com/

Web Site Resources

Forums Freelancers can use

https://forums.digitalpoint.com/
(looking for hire)

http://www.wjunction.com/
(wanted members)

http://www.warriorforum.com/
(warriors for hire)

http://www.talkfreelance.com/

http://www.whydowork.com/

https://studio.envato.com/freelance-switch/

Payment Sites

www.paypal.com

https://home.bluesnap.com/

Web Site Resources

Top Photographer Forums

1. http://www.thephotoforum.com/

2. https://www.dpreview.com/forums/

3. http://photography-on-the.net/forum/

4. http://www.photographycorner.com/forum/

5. https://www.photographytalk.com/forum

6. https://dgrin.com/

7.http://www.theprofessionalphotographyforum.com/forums/

8. http://www.photomacrography.net/forum/

9. http://www.amateurphotographer.co.uk/forums/

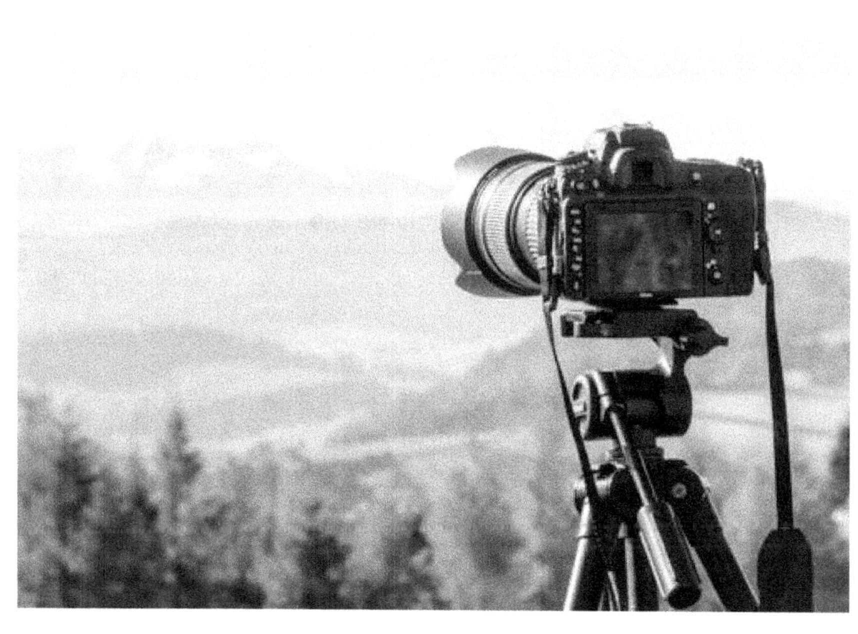

Chapter 12

Photography Terms

Photography Terms

Aperture

A space through which light passes in an optical or photographic instrument, especially the variable opening by which light enters a camera.

Continuous Focus

Continuous Focusing Mode. AI Servo AF (Canon)/AF-C (Nikon) stands for Continuous Focus and this mode is most useful for keeping moving objects sharp within the viewfinder as you track the object.

Aspect Ratio

The ratio of the width to the height of an image or screen.

Bokeh

The visual quality of the out-of-focus areas of a photographic image, especially as rendered by a particular lens.

Photography Terms

Burst Mode

Burst or continuous high speed is a shooting mode i still cameras. In burst mode several photographs ar captured in quick succession by either pressing the shutter button or holding it down. This is used main when the subject is in successive motion, such as sports photography.

Depth of Field

The distance between the nearest and the furthest objects that give an image judged to be in focus in camera.

Digital vs. Optical

The Difference between Optical Zoom and Digital Zoom on Your Digital Camera. ... An optical zoom is true zoom lens, like the zoom lens you'd use on a film camera. They produce much better-quality images. Digital zoom: Some cameras offer a digital zoom, which is simply some in-camera image processing.

Photography Terms

Exposure

In photography, exposure is the amount of light per unit area (the image plane illuminance times the exposure time) reaching a photographic film or electronic image sensor, as determined by shutter speed, lens aperture and scene luminance.

Exposure Compensation

Exposure compensation is the control by which you temporarily adjust your camera's definition of what is "properly exposed". Put simpler, it's a way to force the camera to make your photos darker or brighter to the degree that you tell it.

Focus

the state or quality of having or producing clear visual definition.

Photography Terms

Flash Sync

In a camera, flash synchronization is defined as synchronizing the firing of a photographic flash with the opening of the shutter admitting light to photographic film or electronic image sensor. It is often shortened to flash sync or flash synch.

Histogram

A histogram is a graphical representation of the tonal values of your image. In other words, it shows the amount of tones of particular brightness found in your photograph ranging from black (0% brightness) to white (100% brightness).

Hot Shoe

A hot shoe is a mounting point on the top of a camera to attach a flash unit and other compatible accessories.

Photography Terms

ISO

The lower the ISO number, the less sensitive it is to the light, while a higher ISO number increases the sensitivity of your camera. The component within your camera that can change sensitivity is called "image sensor" or simply "sensor".

Long Exposure

Long-exposure, time-exposure, or slow-shutter photography involves using a long-duration shutter speed to sharply capture the stationary elements of images while blurring, smearing, or obscuring the moving elements.

Manual mode

A or Av: Aperture priority or Aperture value enables manual control of the aperture, and shutter speed is calculated by the camera for proper exposure (given an ISO sensitivity).

Photography Terms

Metering

In photography, the metering mode refers to the way in which a camera determines the exposure.

Noise

Image noise is random (not present in the object imaged) variation of brightness or color information in images, and is usually an aspect of electronic noise. It can be produced by the sensor and circuitry of a scanner or digital camera.

Raw

Image file formats. A camera raw image file contains minimally processed data from the image sensor of either a digital camera, image scanner, or motion picture film scanner. Raw files are named so because they are not yet processed and therefore are not ready to be printed or edited with a bitmap graphics editor.

Photography Terms

Rule of Thirds

The rule of thirds is applied by aligning a subject with the guide lines and their intersection points, placing the horizon on the top or bottom line, or allowing linear features in the image to flow from section to section.

Shutter speed

The time for which a shutter is open at a given setting.

Shutter release

The button on a camera that is pressed to make the shutter open.

Time lapse

Denoting the photographic technique of taking a sequence of frames at set intervals to record changes that take place slowly over time. When the frames are shown at normal speed, or in quick succession, the action seems much faster.

Photography Terms

Viewfinder

A device on a camera showing the field of view of th
lens, used in framing and focusing the picture.

White balance

The color balance on a digital camera.

$10,000

Massive Money Internet Marketing &

Copy Writing & SEO Course &

$1,000 Value Bonus

Internet Marketing Videos

$10,000 MegaSized Internet Marketing & Copy Writing & SEO Course & $1,000 Value Bonus

Library III

1. SEO SIMPLIFIED PART 1

2. SEO SIMPLIFIED PART 2

3. SEO Private Network Blogs

4. SEO Social Signals

5. SEO Profits

Bonus 1000 Package!

1. Insider Secrets to Government Contracts (PDF)

2. 1000 Books/Guides (text files)

3. Vacation Discounts (text file w/links to discounts)

4. Media Players (3 Software Programs)

100% MONEY BACK GUARANTEE!!!

ALL ON A 8 GIGABYTE FLASH DRIVE

This Massive Library with a $10,000 value all for only a

1 time payment of $67!!!

Get Instant Access by Using the Link Below:

https://urlzs.com/p7v3T

Leave a review and join Our VIP Mailing List Then Get All our Audio Books Free!

We will be releasing over 100 money making audio books within the next 12 months! Just leave a review and join our mailing list and get them all for free!

Just Hit/Type in the Link Below

https://urlzs.com/HfbGF

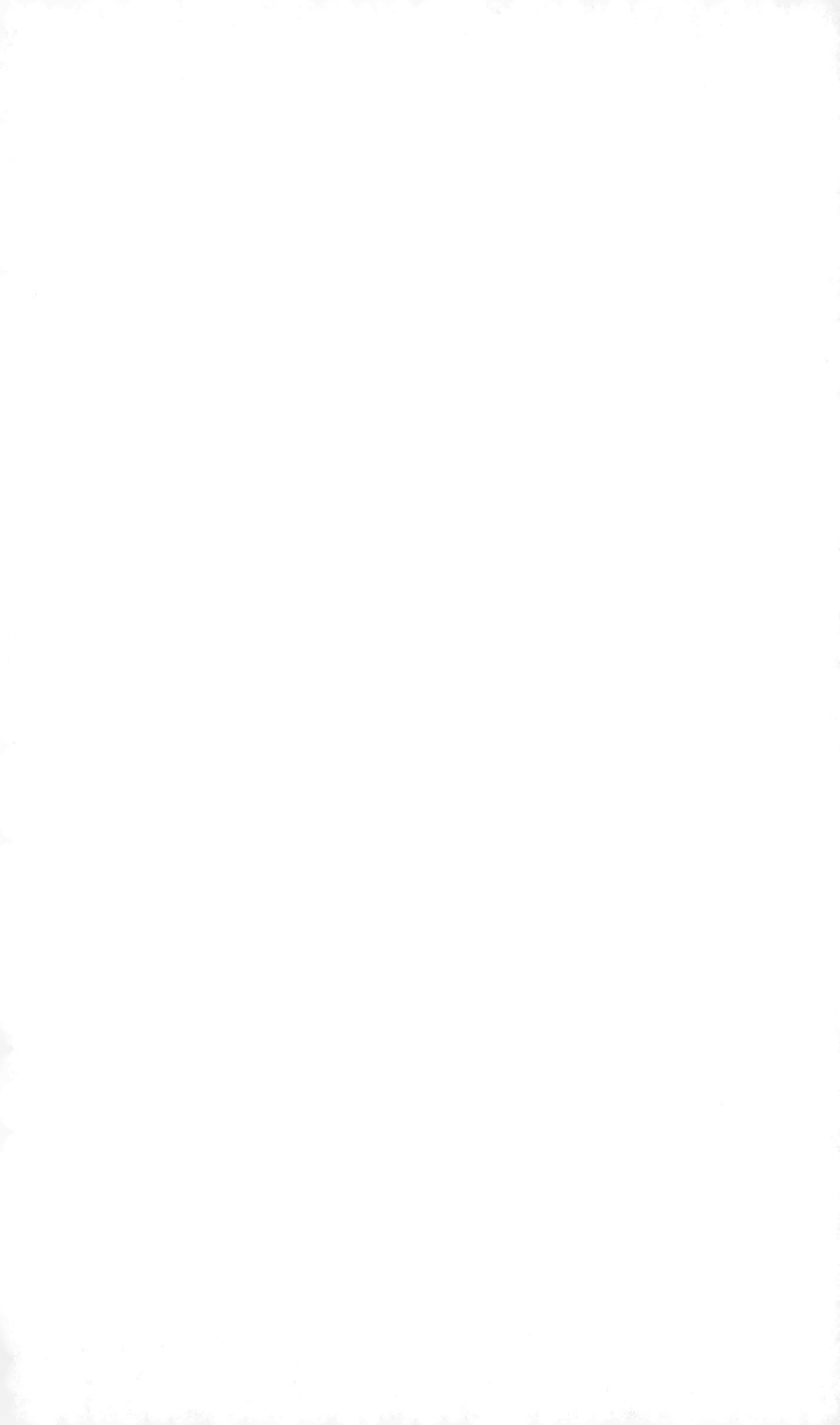

www.ingramcontent.com/pod-product-compliance
Lightning Source LLC
Chambersburg PA
CBHW061735050726
47598CB00002B/492

9 781951 929305